Sports Agent

CAREERS
Off the Field

CAREERS OFF THE FIELD

Analytics: Sports Stats and More

Coaching & Scouting

Health Careers in Sports

Sports Agent

Sports Arena & Event Management

Sports Broadcasting

Sports Marketing

Sports Media Relations

Sportswriting and Sports Photography

Working in College Sports

Sports Agent

By Craig Ellenport

Mason Crest

450 Parkway Drive, Suite D
Broomall, PA 19008
www.masoncrest.com

Printed and bound in the United States of America.

Series ISBN: 978-1-4222-3264-4
Hardback ISBN: 978-1-4222-3270-5
EBook ISBN: 978-1-4222-8528-2

First printing
1 3 5 7 9 8 6 4 2

Produced by Shoreline Publishing Group LLC
Santa Barbara, California
Editorial Director: James Buckley Jr.
Designer: Bill Madrid
Production: Sandy Gordon
www.shorelinepublishing.com
Cover photo by Newscom/Juan DeLeon/Icon SMI
Cover: Top baseball agent Scott Boras with Mark Appel, a star pitcher drafted by the Houston Astros.

Library of Congress Cataloging-in-Publication Data
Ellenport, Craig.
    Sports agent / by Craig Ellenport.
    pages cm. -- (Careers off the field)
    Includes index.   ISBN 978-1-4222-3270-5 (hardback) -- ISBN 978-1-4222-3264-4 (series) -- ISBN 978-1-4222-8528-2 (ebook) 1. Sports agents. I. Title.   GV734.5.E55 2016
796.06'94--dc23
                                        2015007863

CONTENTS

Key Icons to Look For

Words to Understand: These words with their easy-to-understand definitions will increase the reader's understanding of the text, while building vocabulary skills.

Sidebars: This boxed material within the main text allows readers to build knowledge, gain insights, explore possibilities, and broaden their perspectives by weaving together additional information to provide realistic and holistic perspectives.

Research Projects: Readers are pointed toward areas of further inquiry connected to each chapter. Suggestions are provided for projects that encourage deeper research and analysis.

Text-Dependent Questions: These questions send the reader back to the text for more careful attention to the evidence presented here.

Series Glossary of Key Terms: This back-of-the-book glossary contains terminology used throughout this series. Words found here increase the reader's ability to read and comprehend higher-level books and articles in this field.

Foreword

By Al Ferrer

So you want to work in sports? Good luck! You've taken a great first step by picking up this volume of CAREERS OFF THE FIELD. I've been around sports professionally—on and off the field, in the front office, and in the classroom—for more than 35 years. My students have gone on to work in all the major sports leagues and for university athletic programs. They've become agents, writers, coaches, and broadcasters. They were just where you are now, and the lessons they learned can help you succeed.

One of the most important things to remember when looking for a job in sports is that being a sports fan is not enough. If you get an interview with a team, and your first sentence is "I'm your biggest fan," that's a kiss of death. They don't want fans, they want pros. Show your experience, show what you know, show how you can contribute.

Another big no-no is to say, "I'll do anything." That makes you a non-professional or a wanna-be. You have to do the research and find out what area is best for your personality and your skills. This book series will be a vital tool for you to do that research, to find out what areas in sports are out there, what kind of people work in them, and where you would best fit in.

That leads to my third point: Know yourself. Look carefully at your interests and skills. You need to understand what you're good at and how you like to work. If you get energy from being around people, then you don't want to be in a room with a computer because you'll go nuts. You want to be in the action, around people, so you might look at sales or marketing or media relations or being an agent. If you're more comfortable being by yourself, then you look at analysis, research, perhaps the numbers side of scouting or recruiting. You have to know yourself.

You also have to manage your expectations. There is a lot of money in sports, but unless you are a star athlete, you probably won't be making much in your early years.

I'm not trying to be negative, but I want to be realistic. I've loved every minute of my life in sports. If you have a passion for sports and you can bring professionalism and quality work—and you understand your expectations—you can have a great career. Just like the athletes we admire, though, you have to prepare, you have to work hard, and you have to never, ever quit.

Series consultant Al Ferrer founded the sports management program at the University of California, Santa Barbara, after an award-winning career as a Division I baseball coach. Along with his work as a professor, Ferrer is an advisor to pro and college teams, athletes, and sports businesses.

Introduction

When quarterback Warren Moon (yellow jacket, left) was elected to the Pro Football Hall of Fame in 2006, one of the big decisions he had to make leading up to the induction ceremony in Canton, Ohio, was this: Who would he choose to present him?

Before each Hall of Famer is brought to the stage to make a speech in front of the crowd of fans, he chooses someone to say a few words and "present" him for induction into the Hall. Typically, the Hall of Famer might ask his son or daughter to fulfill this great honor. He might choose a coach who had a strong impact on the player's career. It's not uncommon for coaches to be thought of by players as father figures.

Warren Moon went in a different direction. His choice to present him was his agent, Leigh Steinberg.

Of course, Leigh Steinberg isn't just any agent. *Forbes* magazine called him "the greatest sports agent in history." Steinberg represented eight players who were the first overall picks in their respective NFL drafts.

Still, does an agent compare to a coach or family member?

"I knew Leigh was someone special early on," Moon wrote in the foreword to Steinberg's 2014 autobiography—appropriately titled, *The Agent*.

"I am honored that Leigh asked me to write this foreword and am privileged to call Leigh a friend, while, in fact, he has been so much more than that."

While the athletes they represent get all the attention, you usually only hear about sports agents when their clients are looking to sign a new contract. In other words, agents are the ones responsible for your favorite players switching teams, or for your favorite team overpaying for a player you don't think is worth all that money.

The fact of the matter is, a sports agent does much more than negotiate contracts.

"I'm always working the phones—touching base with the clients, touching base with corporate contacts," said Russ Spielman, a partner at The Legacy Agency. "There's always ongoing business. Our clients are doing stuff every week—events, appearances, store openings, commercial shoots. So there's a lot of working on those things—making sure everything is going well.

"Sometimes I feel like an air traffic controller."

Spielman isn't really helping airplanes land, but that might be the only thing he's not doing in his role as agent. In addition to helping clients sign contracts, an agent must do just about

anything to keep the client successful both on the field of play and off.

"We're personal advisors," explained Buddy Baker, the president and chief executive officer for Exclusive Sports Group, the agency he founded. "If there are things that are

Agent Lindsey Kagawa Colas made sure that one of her clients, WNBA star Maya Moore, at left, was at her wedding.

important to them, or if they're going through hard times, you help them navigate those as well."

Baseball agent Page Odle (center) was all smiles when two of his clients finished their college degrees. The best agents share in these life-changing moments.

While Steinberg is a lawyer whose contract negotiating skills are among the best in the business, he has also emphasized to would-be agents who are just getting started that they focus on helping their clients become better people—doing good things in the community and creating foundations to donate both time and money to worthy causes. Like most good agents, he formed a bond with his clients that continued long after their playing days were over.

"We became good friends," Moon wrote about his agent. "He became someone I could talk to about any subject, good and bad, inside and outside of sports. We talked about life and gave each other good advice."

A sports agent is more than a business manager to his or her client. The successful sports agent is a trusted friend.

A statue of football legend Red Grange stands outside the University of Illinois stadium.

Words to Understand

commission: the fee made by an agent; it's a percentage of the value of a client's contract

endorsement: a deal in which a person, in this case an athlete, is paid to promote or help sell a product or service

interns: people who work at jobs for experience rather than pay

Getting Started

CHAPTER 1

The history of the sports agent dates back to 1925, when a theater owner in Illinois named C.C. Pyle helped University of Illinois star running back Red Grange sign a contract to play for the Chicago Bears of the National Football League (NFL). Back then, negotiating contracts was more or less the entire job description for an agent.

Thirty-five years later, a lawyer named Mark McCormack came on the scene and completely transformed the role of sports agent. McCormack, who was an excellent golfer in college, started a company called International Management Group (IMG) in 1960. His first client was a young golfer named Arnold Palmer. McCormack saw the potential for star athletes such as Palmer to earn money not only by competing in sports, but also by signing endorsement deals—starring in commercials, making appearances, and helping companies sell their products.

It didn't hurt that Palmer became one of the greatest golfers in the history of the sport. Over the years, McCormack added several other big names to his list of clients, including Jack Nicklaus, Tiger Woods, Derek Jeter, and Charles Barkley.

There are two things McCormack's clients all had in common:

1) They were winners when competing in their sports; and

2) They were popular enough outside of their sports and maintained an image that made them attractive to advertisers.

It might be safe to say that some of those big-time athletes were already good people and would have been popular enough to succeed off the field without an agent such as McCormack on their side. However, there is no denying the impact he had on their careers. McCormack was the first to put together complete plans for an athlete that included their work on the field and their business lives off the field. How successful was McCormack's vision? Arnold Palmer last won a PGA Tour event in 1973. More than 40 years later, he is still making $40 million a year on product endorsements.

"He was a genius when it came to sports marketing," Tiger Woods said when McCormack passed away on May 16, 2003. "If it wasn't for him, obviously we wouldn't be in the position we are right now."

So how does one become a sports agent? It's not a subject that is taught specifically in high school or college—though many colleges now have sports management programs that can help prepare students for the job.

Super-agent Mark McCormack was a pioneer in the sports agent business.

Education

Postgraduate study is very important. Most agents have degrees from law school or business school. It's not mandatory, but very few agents do not have that experience. In fact, the National Football League Players Association (NFLPA)—which requires agents to become "certified" if they want to represent NFL players—considers very few applicants that do not have both undergraduate and graduate degrees. According to Mark Levin, director of agent administration at the NFLPA, applicants that do not have undergraduate and graduate degrees must have at least seven years of relevant negotiating experience.

Even before the college level, there are things that aspiring sports agents can focus on in high school that will help prepare them for the job.

Agents can't be afraid of a microphone. They need excellent communications and public-speaking skills.

"They have to be well rounded," said Page Odle, a baseball agent who founded the company PSI Sports. "Probably the one area that is most important is really having great communication skills. It all starts with creating that relationship with the athletes. They have to be able to learn how to speak with them. They should also have a very good understanding of the sport that person is playing."

In high school, English is probably the best subject to help with communication skills. If a school has a debate team or a mock trial team, those are excellent ways to improve verbal communication.

"A solid foundation of communication skills doesn't mean just texting with your friends," said Lindsay Kagawa Colas, vice president of action and Olympic sports at Wasserman Media Group. "It means pursuing opportunities to become a better writer and a better speaker—ideally, in more than one language. As an agent, you have to be able to make compelling arguments. Part of that is knowing the answer, but an equally important part is being able to communicate it effectively."

Math is also very important. Dealing with numbers is an everyday part of life as a sports agent. Understanding statistics will help the agent prepare his or her case when trying to negotiate the best contract possible for a client.

Kagawa Colas, like many who get into the business, had no idea she wanted to become an agent until the opportunity presented itself after college. Up to that point, she said, it's important to be well rounded, keep an open mind, and follow your dreams.

"My recommendation for any young person who is intrigued by a career helping others would be to pursue what you are passionate about," she said. "Every agent's background is different. Those differences are what make each agent unique and, often, the right 'fit' for his or her client. There are many routes to becoming an agent."

Once you get to college, whether or not you're in a sports management program, there are a few different directions that can prove helpful.

"It's good to have a business background," said Odle. "You're going to be handling their day-to-day affairs, so having some management and marketing experience is good. Obviously there's a legal side to the business, so young men and women can come into the business from the legal side."

Most colleges offer business classes and prelaw classes. Even if you're not sure if you will go to business school or law school, those undergraduate classes are valuable. Some colleges offer advertising and marketing classes. As the business of being a sports agent has expanded to include such opportunities for clients, knowledge of those subjects will certainly add to your skill set.

Internships

While he isn't minimizing the importance of a good education, sports agent Buddy Baker places even greater emphasis on life experience.

"I don't know there's any specific subject in high school or college that's important," said Baker. "It's more an approach or a mindset."

When Baker attended Purdue University, he worked in the athletic department. It was a full-time job, and even though he didn't get paid for it, the experience was invaluable.

Working for a college athletic department can be a great way to make connections that will help down the road.

"What I would tell a young person who endeavors to be in this field, and I've told all the interns who work here, is that you need to open up your knowledge and your experiences and your contacts," Baker said. "How do you do that? You don't do that by taking certain classes. You do that by trying to get internships, following certain people, shadowing different people, asking questions, researching certain things."

An internship at a sports agency won't get you a seat at the negotiating table. You'll likely be doing more basic tasks, such as making copies, doing research, or even picking up lunch for the office. Still, it is an opportunity to see what an agent does and to learn by observing.

"Watching *SportsCenter* or taking a certain math class isn't going to give you the preparation or the foundation of what you need to be a successful agent," added Baker. "However, going and spending a couple of days at an agency, or learning how things work relevant to the business of sport is much more useful than taking any specific class."

Like Baker's experience at Purdue, any job in a college athletic department would be helpful to an aspiring sports agent. Depending on the size of the school, there can be many needs for athletic volunteers.

In addition to being a good source of information about sports agents in general, the Web site SportsAgentBlog.com has a long list of agencies all over the country that offer internships. See Find Out More, page 62.

Traits and Skills

Successful agents, said Lindsay Kagawa Colas, "are smart, passionate, tenacious, inspiring, creative, committed, and hard working."

Of course, those are traits and not skills. The point is that while you need a strong educational base—math and communication skills, legal and business background—being a sports agent requires mental toughness above all else.

While it's the clients who are competing on the playing field, sports agents face stiff competition of their own. There are so many agents out there, and many of them work for large agencies that have hundreds of clients. A sports agent doesn't earn a base salary—you have to get out there and sign up an athlete before you can make a dime.

Once you do have a client on your roster, the challenge is keeping that client happy. Negotiating the athlete's contract is far from the biggest challenge.

Getting Paid

A sports agent doesn't get paid by the hour, the week, or the year. A sports agent gets paid when his or her client gets paid. Like a salesman, the sports agent gets paid a commission, which is a percentage of the deal that's been arranged for the client.

The unions for players in the National Football League and the National Basketball Association have a rule that limits an agent's compensation to no more than three percent. In other sports, the commission might be between four and ten percent, though the number is closer to four percent in most major sports.

Here's an example. The minimum NFL salary in 2015 was $435,000. So if you sign a college football player who doesn't get drafted but still manages to make an NFL roster, that's what his one-year contract would be worth. Your payday is three percent of $435,000—or $13,050. That's pretty good, but it's also not enough to make a living.

Now let's say you sign a superstar who becomes the tenth overall pick in the draft. Based on recent figures, that player might earn close to $2 million his rookie season. Your three percent commission for that player would be $60,000. That's a much better payday.

That said, there are only 32 first-round NFL draft picks every year, and there are nearly a thousand certified NFL agents trying to sign those players. The competition to sign athletes is as fierce as the battle for jobs on the field.

"I'll put it this way," said Russ Spielman of the Legacy Agency. "The best part of the job is working with the athletes, and the hardest part of the job is working with the athletes.

"We're dealing with people. No two are the same. They have their own unique perspective and circumstances and personal issues and everything like that. We strive to do more. It's a fun, demanding job. And in this modern era you're never off the clock. You're always on the phone, you always have social media going. It's a full-time, twenty-four-hours-a-day, seven-days-a-week job."

Text-Dependent Questions

1. Who does the text credit with starting the modern sports agent business?

2. Postgraduate study: necessary or not?

3. Name three traits or skills the experts say are key to being a sports agent.

Research Project

Who were the top ten athletes in terms of most money earned in 2014 through product endorsements? See if you can find out who their agents were as well. Did those agents represent more than one of the top players? Which agents were with agencies, and which worked solo?

Basketball agent Jeremy Medjana met with his client Evan Fournier after the player was chosen by the Denver Nuggets in the 2014 NBA Draft.

Words to Understand

accountants: professionals who keep track of income and spending for a person or a company

mergers: business deals in which two or more companies combine to form a single, larger company

transactions: in this case, business deals involving the buying or selling of real estate, such as a house

Hard at Work

CHAPTER 2

There is no such thing as a typical day in the life of a sports agent.

For starters, it depends a lot on the time of year and what particular sport an agent is focused on.

If you represent a college basketball player getting ready for the NBA Draft, you might be busy talking to the media, trying to build publicity for your client. When the draft is over and your client has been selected, then contract negotiation becomes the focus.

When the next college season rolls around, it's time to recruit new clients for you or for your agency. That means researching players you might be interested in signing, and contacting those players (as well as friends and family members of those players who might be helping them choose an agent). Being an agent is year-round work, a constant hustle to find new clients and help existing ones.

Much More Than Contracts

Signing new clients is just one part of a busy agent's life. With existing clients, you might have any number of issues to help them with.

- A veteran player may have been released by a team, and you have to help that client sign with a new team.
- The player you signed as a rookie last year had a great first season, so now she needs you to help her get endorsement deals.
- The first athlete you ever signed is nearing the end of his playing career and thinking about life after sports. Whether he wants to become a coach or a broadcaster, or perhaps is looking to start a new business, he is leaning on his agent for help.

Of course, many other unforeseen issues might come up. Family trouble? Money trouble? Buying the right car? It's not unusual for a sports agent to be the first person called for such things.

"I handle business affairs for most of my clients," said baseball agent Page Odle. "I'm so engulfed in their lives that they lean on me to buy and lease cars, to help them in real estate transactions, to help them find good accountants and people

Agents have to be well-versed in contract language and be ready to explain deal points to their clients.

to assist in their lives…There's a lot that most people probably don't understand. That's really a big part of it. The contract side of it is really a small part of being an agent."

The Clients' Generation

Unless you begin your career as a sports agent before graduating college, the one constant is that your clients will almost always be younger than you. That means your client often will look up to you and seek your guidance.

Agent Buddy Baker looks over contract paperwork with NFL defensive end Mike DeVito (right).

"Besides being passionate, you have to have great people skills," said sports agent Buddy Baker. "You have to know how to give advice, how to react, how to deal with people from

different backgrounds. You have to understand that you're a leader of men and women—young men and women—and help them make good business decisions, help them make good life decisions.

"Being a successful agent, in some ways you're not just a role model. More than that, you're a counselor. You're a counselor from a business standpoint, and you're a counselor professionally. I think those are some of the core characteristics of being a good agent."

Build Your Contacts

When Baker decided to become a sports agent, he already had been a successful lawyer who just happened to have experience working in athletics. So the first thing he did was make a list of potential contacts.

"It's a relationship-driven business," Baker said. "I put down on paper every relevant contact I had in the world of sports—whether it was a coach, somebody in management, a player, etcetera—and tried to put together an action plan that could build my contacts and potentially help me find a player. And that's what I did. I just started getting in touch with everybody and letting them know what I was doing."

Communication is the key. Agents need to use all the connections at their disposal in order to find new recruits.

Leigh Steinberg wasn't the only agent who was recruiting University of Washington quarterback Warren Moon after the future Pro Football Hall of Fame member was named MVP of the 1978 Rose Bowl. However, when Moon received a letter from Steinberg asking if they could meet, he learned something about Steinberg that set him apart from the other agents: Steinberg was a graduate of Hamilton High School in Los Angeles—same as Moon. They had common ground.

"We always look for where there's some sort of commonality," said Baker. "Have we represented a player from that school? Is there somebody they know that knows us?"

Changing Face of Agencies

Kenny Zuckerman's company, Priority Sports & Entertainment, employs several sports agents who used to work independently. That's part of a trend that began in the 1990s and has really changed the business of sports agents.

For a variety of reasons, some agents realized they would be stronger if they merged their businesses. "Most of the mergers [among sports agencies] that you see are people that are not

Jobs at a Sports Agency

When Kenny Zuckerman began working at Priority Sports & Entertainment in 1999, there were five people in the office. They had to do everything—all the little things that went into building the agency. Today, Priority employs 30 people and has offices in Chicago and Los Angeles.

That growth allows Zuckerman and the other agents in the company to focus on the bigger picture of getting contracts done. That means there are several other full-time employees who—while not considered agents—are very important to the agency.

"They are your support system," explained Zuckerman. "You need somebody to handle travel, somebody to handle endorsements, somebody to handle marketing, shoe deals, trading-card deals. We have somebody who does all those different things."

Of course, you also must have a lot of clients to staff your office like that.

"An agent dealing with a one- or two- or three-person office, even if they're dealing with only five clients, they're swamped with so many little things," said Zuckerman.

One thing for an aspiring agent to consider: There might be more opportunities to learn the business doing one of those support jobs at a bigger agency. When you feel you are ready to become an agent, you might branch out on your own or perhaps get promoted at the bigger company.

getting to where they want to go on their own," said Zuckerman. "So they feel there might be strength in numbers, to give the appearance of a larger company."

In other cases, the new agency model came about because of the way sports and entertainment have come together.

International soccer superstar David Beckham and his agents used his athletic fame to sign many endorsement deals, including clothing.

Creative Artists Agency (CAA) has been one of the biggest talent agencies in Hollywood since the 1970s, representing top names in music, TV, and movies. In 2006, CAA decided to get into the sports business, using its entertainment connections as a way to lure big-name sports stars. After all, if CAA had all these connections in the entertainment business, couldn't it get appearances in commercials or on TV shows for its top-notch sports clients? As of 2015, CAA's sports division represented stars such as Derek Jeter, Peyton Manning,

Derek Jeter built a great reputation as a player. Now in retirement, he and his agents will have different ways to take advantage of that good name.

and David Beckham—all very recognizable faces in the sports and entertainment worlds.

It's hard for an independent agent to compete with a company such as CAA, which has an army of employees to help its agents handle the business. However, the need to provide more for athletes beyond the playing field has certainly changed the way all agents approach the job.

Big agent or small, the key to success is a balancing act between the search for new clients and the time it takes to keep existing clients happy.

Agent Kenny Zuckerman went shoe shopping with his son and his football-playing client, quarterback Brett Hundley.

"Your clients are your lifeline," said sports agent Buddy Baker. "We look at our existing clients more than our prospective clients. We're always looking for new players, obviously, but if you're going to be truly successful—if you want to be regarded as elite in your industry, a professional in your industry—then you have to concentrate on reacting to your current clients' needs."

Text-Dependent Questions

1. What are two other sorts of deals an agent might help a client with, besides the contract with a team?
2. What did Buddy Baker advise future agents to build?
3. What did the sidebar suggest was another way into an agency?

Research Project

Imagine you are an agent. Find five college athletes you would contact to see if you can represent them. What is the connection that might make them interested? Write a one-page "pitch letter" offering your services and ideas to one of those athletes.

Former soccer star Landon Donovan (left) invited his longtime agent Richard Motzkin to the ceremony naming the MLS MVP award for Donovan.

Words to Understand

bylaws: rules created inside an organization, as opposed to laws created by a government

credibility: the ability to be believed and trusted

due diligence: the process of studying all aspects of a situation before making a decision

ethical: acting in a way that follows the rules and does the right things

incentives: parts of a contract that award extra pay for reaching certain levels or achieving certain goals

ineligible: unable to take part due to having broken rules

Realities of the Workplace

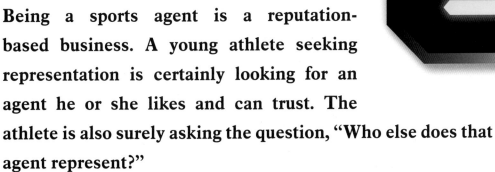

CHAPTER 3

Being a sports agent is a reputation-based business. A young athlete seeking representation is certainly looking for an agent he or she likes and can trust. The athlete is also surely asking the question, "Who else does that agent represent?"

It's a chicken-and-egg problem, but the bottom line is this: The more clients you represent, the better chance you have of attracting new clients. If you're just starting out, it's important to have others in the industry who can vouch for you.

"We feel we provide a very high level of service in this industry, but anyone can say those words," said agent Buddy Baker. "How do you distinguish yourself? You look for somebody who can give you some credibility as to who you are, who your agency is, what you've done. That's the first thing."

Basketball coach Cuonzo Martin relied on agent Buddy Baker when he took the job at UC Berkeley.

You have to build your brand. Successful agents have their own Web sites that include information about who they are and whom they represent. Their sites are an opportunity to sell potential new clients on all the great things they can do for them.

Baker's agency, Exclusive Sports Group, has a section on its site called "Testimonials," in which you can read what various people have to say about the agency. Some quotes are from clients. Others are from team coaches and general managers.

Kenny Zuckerman's agency, Priority Sports & Entertainment, has a site that features several highly produced videos, with Zuckerman and other members of the company talking about the different things they do to help their clients. The videos include plenty of images of framed jerseys with hand-written notes from athletes thanking Zuckerman and his partners for their great work.

Agent Kenny Zuckerman helped his client, college defensive star Nate Orchard (8, below), prepare for the 2015 NFL Draft.

Making Connections

Advances in technology have made it much easier these days to contact potential clients. Thirty years ago, Leigh Steinberg mailed a letter to Warren Moon. Agents today can cover much more ground now via email or text.

Of course, no athlete is going to pick an agent based on a letter, email, or phone call. The intent of that first contact is to:

- introduce yourself to the athlete;
- let him or her know that you are interested in helping them;
- set up a meeting.

Some agents prefer to be more direct by introducing themselves to athletes in person. Colleges have some restrictions in place for the amount of contact athletes can have with agents, but they are allowed to have some interaction.

Zuckerman recalled the days when he used to attend many college football games trying to meet potential clients. He doesn't do that anymore.

"We don't show up at a game and say hello to a player outside the locker room," he said. "It's no longer like that in our business. It used to be. It used to be I'd show up at a game, and outside the locker room there'd be four or five agents coming to see that one player."

Now, said Zuckerman, all business with potential new clients is done with scheduled meetings.

When you secure that first meeting with a potential client, you need to present a solid business plan, showing the athlete

Agents need to be able to present themselves and their business plan well, to entice future clients and their families.

you have a direction for how you will guide his or her career. It's even more important, though, to strike a good relationship with the athlete—or at least begin to develop that relationship.

"We have to build the relationship," said Baker. "And that isn't one call or two calls or a two-hour meeting. What we tell families and players is to make a decision after investing a lot of time and energy. If they do their **due diligence**, they'll get to know you personally and professionally. Hopefully, as they go through that, you're able to provide them with better understanding, and you're gaining better credibility. Along the way, you're letting the clients know the things you can do for them."

NCAA Rules

A story in *SPORT* magazine in 1993 described the experience Pro Football Hall of Fame running back Marshall Faulk had with agents when he was an underclassman at San Diego State. When he was a sophomore, an agent approached Faulk in the middle of a team practice to discuss a line of clothing. Another agent followed Faulk to the cleaners and cornered him, telling him how much money he would give him if he signed with him. The story also mentioned former NFL receiver Qadry Ismail, who played for Syracuse University in the early 1990s. Ismail referred all agents to Dr. Malcolm

Things have changed a lot since former NFL star Marshall Faulk was in college.

Conway, a family friend who served as a personal trainer and advisor to Ismail. Dr. Conway quickly became well acquainted with the agent business. He lumped agents into three categories.

"There are the heavyweights, who know what they're doing," said Dr. Conway. "There are the guys in the middle who are trying to make a name for themselves, and they're hustling. And then there are the guys out there that I consider sleazy. There's a ton of them out there."

Fortunately for all involved, the industry has changed drastically since the 1990s, as both colleges and state governments have taken added measures to protect college athletes from the "sleazy" agents who do not operate in an ethical manner.

Before reaching out to a college athlete, it's critical to understand the rules in place about how an agent can contact these athletes. The National Collegiate Athletic Association (NCAA) has bylaws in place, and there are some states that have their own actual laws in place.

If college athletes sign or have improper contact with an agent, they can become ineligible and lose their scholarship. The school can get penalized as well, which is why coaches and other athletic department administrators are charged with looking out for their athletes' best interests.

In 2000, the Uniform Athlete Agents Act (UAAA) was created to define the ways in which agents can interact with college athletes. Many states recognize and support the UAAA, while some states have their own laws regulating agents.

Getting Certified

Earning the trust and confidence of a potential client is critical. In some cases, there are other requirements that must be met before you can represent an athlete.

In order to represent athletes in most team sports, agents often are required to be "certified" by the league's union. That way, the organization can keep track of agents, making sure they are professionals who understand the complexities of the job. Without this regulation, anyone could claim to be an agent and perhaps cheat a prospective client out of his or her money. It also helps to be certified because college players might reach out to leagues for a list of certified agents. An agent would need to be on that list to get clients.

Of course, getting certified is an investment. The National Football League Players Association (NFLPA), for example, charges an application fee of $2,500 to become a certified football agent. Agents must also pass a test—answering questions about negotiating, NFL team policies, and other related subjects—to become certified. After passing the test and paying the application fee, agents still must pay annual dues to remain certified. Dues can range from $1,500 to $2,000 per year, depending on how many clients an agent has.

Believe it or not, there are many agents who pay to become certified and still don't have any clients. They are hoping to land that one big client who will make it all worthwhile— but it can't be done unless they are already certified.

Most years, there are nearly 900 agents certified by the NFLPA. According to Andrew Brandt, a former agent who now covers the business of football for ESPN, almost half of them had no clients. Some

Scott Boras has become one of the most powerful agents in baseball in his more than 35 years of work.

agents have one or two clients. Meanwhile, there are a handful of conglomerates that represent a majority of athletes. In pro football, Creative Artists Agency (CAA) and Rosenhaus Sports represent more than 100 players each.

Negotiating Contracts

Negotiating contracts is still one of the most important things an agent does. It requires a great deal of preparation, knowledge of the marketplace, bargaining skills, and a thorough understanding of what your client wants.

Contracts are not always about the money. It's important to know the proper language and how to structure the deal. In addition to a salary and signing bonus, contracts might include incentives—extra money if the

Agents who are not also lawyers often get added legal help when drafting client contracts.

Working With the Unions

When Mark Levin worked for the Washington Redskins, he used to sit on the opposite side of the negotiating table with players and their agents. He saw firsthand how some agents were simply unprepared for negotiating major contracts with professional sports teams. In his current job as director of agent administration for the NFL Players Association (NFLPA), Levin's mission is to help NFL players avoid getting stuck with bad agents.

This is done two ways. First, the NFLPA requires that an agent be certified in order to represent an NFL player. Being certified requires clearing a background check, passing a test, and paying annual dues.

"The NFL has agreed that they will only negotiate player contracts with people that we say are certified," said Levin. "Players want agents who are serious about the business and do this full time. Once they're certified, they still have to come to one seminar every year."

The second way the NFLPA helps is by helping certified agents do their jobs. "You have access as an agent to salary information," said Levin. "We run a bunch of different salary reports, we have copies of every player contract. We're also here to help them negotiate the contracts. A lot of agents just rely on us for information purposes, but some agents really lean on us for advice and guidance in negotiating the contract."

Other major sports with unions for their players have similar models in place to regulate and help agents. After all, the unions want what's best for their players. That means good agents.

athlete attains certain goals. You should know what's important to your client, and what the client thinks he or she can do.

When negotiations begin, some clients might want to be very involved; others will rely on you to get the best deal possible.

Baseball agent Page Odle proudly posed with client James Shields after the pitcher signed a new contract with the San Diego Padres.

Either way, it's important for you to keep the lines of communication open and to make sure that the client always knows what's going on.

Negotiations aren't always easy. While you are trying to get the best deal possible for your client, the team's executives also are trying to get the best deal possible for the team. Eventually, the deal gets done—but it's not all smooth sailing.

"It's important to keep your composure at all times," said baseball agent Page Odle. "When you're talking large amounts of money, there can be times when things get heated and there are disagreements.

"I just really pride myself on always staying professional. I just remind myself this is never about me—it's about my client and what's best for him."

Text-Dependent Questions

1. How do agents connect with athletes today? What is one way they don't use any more?

2. What is the name of the process an agent must go through before he or she can represent an NFL player?

3. About what percent of agents, according to ESPN, have no clients?

Research Project

Research the Uniform Athlete Agents Act (UAAA) and make a list of five things agents are allowed to do and five things they are not allowed to do when contacting college athletes.

Words to Understand

marketable: able to be hired to do endorsements

proactively: working on your own without getting initial direction; acting first instead of waiting for others

prospect: an athlete the experts feel has a shot at becoming a professional

supplements: vitamins and other food that athletes take to help them train

The Nitty-Gritty

CHAPTER 4

While an agent's job requires working closely with millionaires, don't expect to become an agent and get rich overnight. The reality is quite the opposite, in many cases.

"When kids call me and say they want to be in the business, I tell them it's harder to become a sports agent than an actor," said Kenny Zuckerman of Priority Sports & Entertainment. "It really is. Because in football, I would say there are probably three or four agents that make over $1 million a year. Maybe five. There are probably ten total that make $500,000 a year, and maybe twenty-five that make over $250,000. And that's out of the hundreds of agents that are certified." (An example of the high-end agent is David Falk, pictured at left with NBA client Elton Brand.) Money shouldn't be the driving factor. For most successful agents, it's not.

"I'm driven by the relationship part, mentoring young men and helping them through this journey," said baseball agent Page Odle. "The greatest days of my life are the days young men get called up to the major leagues for the first time, and they're there with their family and their loved ones."

Investing Time and Money

Odle had the advantage of being a former baseball player himself. Having played in the Pittsburgh Pirates' minor-league system,

he knew how hard it was for any prospect—no matter how highly regarded—to make it all the way up to the majors. For that reason, Odle feels the need to offer his clients many services that will help them on their journey—services that Odle pays for.

To make sure their young clients are ready to impress the pros, agents often pay for training sessions.

"Before they make it to the major leagues, I might spend six or seven years with a young man, and invest a lot of money in him," said Odle. "Helping him pay for training, supplements— those are my commitments back to them, and they do not pay me that money back unless they get to the major leagues."

Baseball isn't the only sport in which an agent must invest in off-the-field training and nutrition. Olympic and other amateur sports in particular might require more of an investment from the agent. Here's a list of things an agent might have to pay for before and during a client's career:

- Predraft workout prep
- Wardrobe (draft outfits for players at the NBA and NFL drafts are usually covered by agents)
- Nutritionist
- Web site design
- Digital/social media consulting
- Speaking/media training
- Bookkeeping services
- Travel (for agent or staff) to work with the athlete during appearances, media, meetings, and competition
- Travel (for athlete) to see specialists to get opinions on injuries

Million Dollar Arm

Even though agents must spend a good deal of their time working on contracts and other business projects, creativity remains an important part of the job. Agents must be able to "think outside the box" to come up with new ways to help their clients—and themselves. J.B. Bernstein is a perfect example of this. Bernstein became a successful agent in the 1990s, representing superstars such as NFL running back Barry Sanders and baseball slugger Barry Bonds. As his big-name clients retired from professional sports, Bernstein struggled to keep his business going. He needed to try something new.

That's when Bernstein came up with the idea for *Million Dollar Arm*, a reality TV show based in India, home to a nation of cricket-loving athletes. Bernstein created an *American Idol*-type search in which the winning cricket bowler had a chance to come to America and try out with a Major League Baseball team at pitching. Eventually, Bernstein discovered two 17-year-olds, Rinku Singh and Dinesh Patel, both of whom came to the United States and signed with the Pittsburgh Pirates. Patel has since returned to India, but Singh was still in the Pirates' minor-league system in 2015.

For Bernstein, the success isn't the money he might earn as Singh's agent. More significant is the fact that the story of *Million Dollar Arm* was turned into a successful Disney movie—with Hollywood star Jon Hamm playing Bernstein.

Also, as baseball becomes more popular in India, there will eventually be more chances for players from that country to reach the pros. So when they're looking for an agent, who better to sign with than Bernstein?

Whether it's investing in services to improve an athlete's performance or just taking care of the client's day-to-day needs, there really is no limit to an agent's job description.

"Part of being an agent is never saying, 'That's not my job,'" said Wasserman Media Group's Lindsay Kagawa Colas, who represents Olympic athletes and some of the biggest names in the WNBA. "My relationship with my clients is very personal. When I sign a client, I am committed to her personal development as an athlete and as a person. In doing that, I accept the responsibility of making sure that client has what she needs to be successful.

"Sometimes, that's negotiating a great contract, and other times it might be relationship advice or helping somebody plan a wedding proposal. No day is the same, and the best agents know that it's all about service where clients come first."

Expanding the Role

The huge growth of the sports business as a whole has created more opportunities for the agent. There are so many more ways for athletes today to continue to be successful long after their playing days. The ever-expanding media industry has created new jobs for athletes as broadcasters on TV, radio, and the Internet. Even while a client is in the middle of his or her playing career and the focus is on contract negotiations, the agent must keep an eye toward the future.

Priority Sports & Entertainment created a division not too long ago just for coaches and broadcasters. Rick Smith, who was one of its football agents, now works almost exclusively on coach contracts. Former NBA stars such as Steve Kerr and Danny Manning, who were represented by Priority Sports as players, are now represented by Priority Sports as coaches.

"Playing pro football is not your career," said football agent Kenny Zuckerman. "It's a stepping-stone to your real career. And for somebody to be successful, you have to prepare for life after football now. You have to plan."

In fact, "PLAN" is the acronym for the program Zuckerman's agency put in place for its clients: Prepare for Life After football Now. The agency will bring in different people from

Steve Kerr went from NBA player to NBA coach. Throughout the process, he was guided by his agent's plan.

various businesses to talk to its clients and give them a taste of what it's like to work in that business.

"You have to maximize your relationships and your opportunities playing pro football to set yourself up for your next career," said Zuckerman.

Smaller agencies or independent agents might not be equipped to manage the kind of work that clients might get after their playing days—endorsements, event appearances, etc. Some agents prefer to focus only on representing athletes and coaches after they're done competing. For example, the Legacy Agency does represent some current athletes, but its focus is on players and coaches no longer active in their sports.

"We have a whole different niche of the business that most people probably don't even know exists," said Russ Spielman of the Legacy Agency. "Our business is more of an art than a science."

Rather than waiting for a company to call asking for an athlete to appear in a commercial, Spielman will proactively think of ideas he can pitch to companies.

"We always look for something—whatever that one thing may be that makes them marketable," said Spielman. "Are they great off the field? Is it their personality? Their physical appearance? What is it that makes them someone that is significant—that is potentially marketable?"

Giving Back

So many professional athletes look to give back to their communities with youth camps, fundraising events, or year-round charitable foundations. These are no small undertakings—and of course they are yet another responsibility of the agent.

While it's not easy, it does provide agents with a sense of accomplishment and the ability to know that they've done their part in helping people.

"I am really passionate about the power of sports, and I've always been drawn to social justice issues," said Lindsay Kagawa Colas. "My work as an agent, advocating for my clients and helping them to find their voice, achieve their potential, and be a role model for others really marries those two interests."

A good sports agent will work between 60 and 80 hours a week, and between email and cell phones, he or she is never really off the clock.

It's not an easy job, but the chance to be part of a successful athlete's team can be highly rewarding both professionally and personally.

Helping a client promote a high-profile media event can be part of an agent's work. Here, WNBA star Maya Moore appears with President Obama at the White House.

Text-Dependent Questions

1. Name three things an agent might have to pay for until a client is signed by a team.

2. Where did J.B. Bernstein go to find new clients?

3. About how many agents does the text say make more than $250,000 per year?

Research Project

Imagine you represent an all-star basketball player who is interested in making money in endorsement deals. Come up with five ideas to pitch to different companies, such as ad campaigns they can run using your client.

Find Out More

Books

Shropshire, Kenneth L. and Timothy Davis. *The Business of Sports Agents*. Philadelphia: University of Pennsylvania Press, 2013.

Steinberg, Leigh. *The Agent: My 40-Year Career Making Deals and Changing the Game*. New York: Thomas Dunne Books, 2014.

Web Sites

Exclusive Sports
exclusivesg.com

NFL Players' Association (Agent Rules Page)
nflpa.com/about/rules-and-regulations

PSI Sports
www.psisports.com

Sports Agent Blog
www.sportsagentblog.com

Wasserman Media
www.wmgllc.com

Series Glossary of Key Terms

academic: relating to classes and studies

alumni: people who graduate from a particular college

boilerplate: a standard set of text and information that an organization puts at the end of every press release

compliance: the action of following rules

conferences: groups of schools that play each other frequently in sports

constituencies: a specific group of people related by their connection to an organization or demographic group

credential: a document that gives the holder permission to take part in an event in a way not open to the public

eligibility: a student's ability to compete in sports, based on grades or other school or NCAA requirements

entrepreneurs: people who start their own companies

freelance: a person who does not work full-time for a company, but is paid for each piece of work

gamer: in sports journalism, a write-up of a game

intercollegiate: something that takes places between two schools, such as a sporting event

internships: positions that rarely offer pay but provide on-the-job experience

objective: material written based solely on the facts of a situation

orthopedics: the branch of medicine that specializes in preventing and correcting problems with bones and muscles

recruiting: the process of finding the best athletes to play for a team

revenue: money earned from a business or event

spreadsheets: computer programs that calculate numbers and organize information in rows and columns

subjective: material written from a particular point of view, choosing facts to suit the opinion

Index

Credits

About the Author

Craig Ellenport is a veteran sports journalist who has written about and covered the NFL, NBA, NHL, college football, and Major League Baseball. Craig is coeditor of *The Super Bowl: An Official Retrospective* and a frequent contributor to the annual Super Bowl Game Program. He lives in North Massapequa, N.Y., with his wife and two sons.